Gratitude Journal

BELONGS TO:

● ●

5 Minutes a Day
to Cultivate
Gratitude, Mindfulness
and
Productivity

My goals for the next 90 days

_____

_____

_____

_____

_____

_____

_____

_____

_____

My thoughts and plans

_____

_____

_____

_____

_____

_____

_____

THIS MONTHS PLAN

My goals for month 1

_____

_____

_____

_____

_____

_____

_____

'Believe you can and you're halfway there'
Theodore Roosevelt

How I will improve myself

_____

_____

_____

_____

_____

_____

Something fun I will do this month

_____

_____

Date

____/____/____

1. _____

2. _____

3. _____

TODAY I FEEL :   😊   😐   ☹️

How will I make today amazing ?

_____

_____

_____

"The only thing that is ultimately real about your journey is the step that you are taking at this moment. That's all there ever is."
- Sylvia Boorstein

Todays moments of joy

_____

_____

How could I have made today better

_____

_____

1 Simple goal for tomorrow

_____

Date

____/____/____

TODAY I AM GRATEFUL FOR

1. _____

2. _____

3. _____

TODAY I FEEL : ☺ 😐 ☹

How will I make today amazing ?

_____

_____

"Meditation is to be aware of what is going on: in your body,
in your feelings, in your mind, and in the world."
- Eckhart Tolle

Todays moments of joy

_____

_____

How could I have made today better

_____

_____

1 Simple goal for tomorrow

Date

_____/_____/_____

TODAY I AM GRATEFUL FOR

1. _____

2. _____

3. _____

TODAY I FEEL : ☺ 😐 ☹

How will I make today amazing ?

_____

_____

"Mindfulness isn't difficult, we just need to remember to do it."
- Sharon Salzberg

Todays moments of joy

_____

_____

How could I have made today better

_____

_____

1 Simple goal for tomorrow

_____

Date
_____/_____/_____

TODAY I AM GRATEFUL FOR

1. _____
2. _____
3. _____

TODAY I FEEL :   ☺   😐   ☹

How will I make today amazing ?

_____
_____

"Walk as if you are kissing the Earth with your feet."
- Thich Nhat Hanh

Todays moments of joy

_____
_____

How could I have made today better

_____
_____

1 Simple goal for tomorrow

_____

Date
_____/_____/_____

TODAY I AM GRATEFUL FOR

1. _____
2. _____
3. _____

TODAY I FEEL : ☺ 😐 ☹

How will I make today amazing ?

_____
_____

"Every time we become aware of a thought, as opposed to being lost in a thought, we experience that opening of the mind."
- Joseph Goldstein

Todays moments of joy

_____
_____

How could I have made today better

_____
_____

1 Simple goal for tomorrow

Date
____/____/____

TODAY I AM GRATEFUL FOR

1. _____

2. _____

3. _____

TODAY I FEEL :   ☺   😐   ☹

How will I make today amazing ?

_____

_____

"Feelings come and go like clouds in a windy sky. Conscious breathing is my anchor."
- Thich Nhat Hanh

Todays moments of joy

_____

How could I have made today better

_____

1 Simple goal for tomorrow

_____

Date

____/____/____

TODAY I AM GRATEFUL FOR

1. _____

2. _____

3. _____

TODAY I FEEL :   ☺   😐   ☹

How will I make today amazing ?

_____

_____

"The greatest communication is usually how we are rather than what we say."
- Joseph Goldstein

Todays moments of joy

_____

_____

How could I have made today better

_____

_____

1 Simple goal for tomorrow

_____

Date

____/____/____

TODAY I AM GRATEFUL FOR

1. _____

2. _____

3. _____

TODAY I FEEL : ☺ 😐 ☹

How will I make today amazing ?

_____

_____

"Wherever you are, be there totally."
- Eckhart Tolle

Todays moments of joy

_____

_____

How could I have made today better

_____

_____

1 Simple goal for tomorrow

_____

Date
____/____/____

TODAY I AM GRATEFUL FOR

1. _____
2. _____
3. _____

TODAY I FEEL : ☺ 😐 ☹

How will I make today amazing ?

_____
_____

"What you are looking for is what is looking."
- Joseph Goldstein

Todays moments of joy

_____
_____

How could I have made today better

_____
_____

1 Simple goal for tomorrow

_____

Date
____/____/____

TODAY I AM GRATEFUL FOR

1. _____
2. _____
3. _____

TODAY I FEEL :   ☺   😐   ☹

How will I make today amazing ?

_____
_____
_____

"Do every act of your life as though it were the last act of your life."
- Marcus Aurelius

Todays moments of joy

_____

How could I have made today better

_____

1 Simple goal for tomorrow

_____

Date
____/____/____

TODAY I AM GRATEFUL FOR

1. _____

2. _____

3. _____

TODAY I FEEL : ☺ 😐 ☹

How will I make today amazing ?

_____

_____

"If you miss the present moment, you miss your appointment with life. That is very serious!"
- Thich Nhat Hanh

Todays moments of joy

_____

_____

How could I have made today better

_____

_____

1 Simple goal for tomorrow

_____

Date

____/____/____

TODAY I AM GRATEFUL FOR

1. _____

2. _____

3. _____

TODAY I FEEL :   🙂   😐   🙁

How will I make today amazing ?

_____

_____

"Meditate ... do not delay, lest you later regret it."
- The Buddha

Todays moments of joy

_____

How could I have made today better

_____

1 Simple goal for tomorrow

_____

Date
____/____/____

TODAY I AM GRATEFUL FOR

1. _____
2. _____
3. _____

TODAY I FEEL :   ☺   😐   ☹

How will I make today amazing ?

_____
_____

"Mindful and creative, a child who has neither a past, nor examples to follow, nor value judgments, simply lives, speaks and plays in freedom."
- Arnaud Desjardins

Todays moments of joy

_____
_____

How could I have made today better

_____
_____

1 Simple goal for tomorrow

_____

Date
_____/_____/_____

TODAY I AM GRATEFUL FOR

1. _____

2. _____

3. _____

TODAY I FEEL :   😊   😐   ☹️

How will I make today amazing ?

_____

_____

"You can't stop the waves, but you can learn to surf."
- Jon Kabat-Zinn

Todays moments of joy

_____

_____

How could I have made today better

_____

_____

1 Simple goal for tomorrow

_____

Date
____/____/____

TODAY I AM GRATEFUL FOR

1. _____
2. _____
3. _____

TODAY I FEEL : ☺ 😐 ☹

How will I make today amazing ?

_____
_____
_____

"Until we can manage time, we can manage nothing else."
Peter Drucker

Todays moments of joy

_____
_____

How could I have made today better

_____
_____

1 Simple goal for tomorrow

_____

Date

____/____/____

TODAY I AM GRATEFUL FOR

1. _____

2. _____

3. _____

TODAY I FEEL :   ☺   😐   ☹

How will I make today amazing ?

_____

_____

_____

"Amateurs sit and wait for inspiration, the rest of us just get up and go to work."
Stephen King

Todays moments of joy

_____

_____

How could I have made today better

_____

_____

1 Simple goal for tomorrow

_____

Date
____/____/____

TODAY I AM GRATEFUL FOR

1. _____
2. _____
3. _____

TODAY I FEEL :   ☺   😐   ☹

How will I make today amazing ?

_____
_____
_____

"If you spend too much time thinking about a thing, you'll never get it done."
Bruce Lee

Todays moments of joy

_____

How could I have made today better

_____
_____

1 Simple goal for tomorrow

_____

Date
_____/_____/_____

TODAY I AM GRATEFUL FOR

1. _____

2. _____

3. _____

TODAY I FEEL : ☺ 😐 ☹

How will I make today amazing ?

_____

_____

"It's not knowing what to do, it's doing what you know."
Tony Robbins

Todays moments of joy

_____

How could I have made today better

_____

1 Simple goal for tomorrow

_____

Date
____/____/____

TODAY I AM GRATEFUL FOR

1. _____
2. _____
3. _____

TODAY I FEEL :   ☺   😐   ☹

How will I make today amazing ?

_____
_____
_____

"When you do something, you should burn yourself up completely, like a good bonfire, leaving no trace of yourself."
- Shunryu Suzuki

Todays moments of joy

_____

How could I have made today better

_____

1 Simple goal for tomorrow

_____

Date
____/____/____

TODAY I AM GRATEFUL FOR

1. _____

2. _____

3. _____

TODAY I FEEL : :) :| :(

How will I make today amazing ?

_____

_____

"Practice is this life, and realization is this life, and this life is revealed right here and now."
- Maezumi Roshi

Todays moments of joy

_____

_____

How could I have made today better

_____

_____

1 Simple goal for tomorrow

_____

Date
_____/_____/_____

TODAY I AM GRATEFUL FOR

1. _____
2. _____
3. _____

TODAY I FEEL :   ☺   ☹   ☹

How will I make today amazing ?

_____
_____

"Emotion arises at the place where mind & body meet. It is
the body's reaction to mind."
- Eckhart Tolle

Todays moments of joy

_____

How could I have made today better

_____

1 Simple goal for tomorrow

_____

Date
_____/_____/_____

TODAY I AM GRATEFUL FOR

1. _____
2. _____
3. _____

TODAY I FEEL :   😊   😐   ☹️

How will I make today amazing ?

_____
_____
_____

"Use every distraction as an object of meditation and they
cease to be distractions."
- **Mingyur Rinpoche**

Todays moments of joy

_____

How could I have made today better

_____

1 Simple goal for tomorrow

_____

Date
____/____/____

TODAY I AM GRATEFUL FOR

1. _____
2. _____
3. _____

TODAY I FEEL :   ☺   😐   ☹

How will I make today amazing ?

_____
_____
_____

"Happiness is your nature. It is not wrong to desire it. What
is wrong is seeking it outside when it is inside."
- Ramana Maharshi

Todays moments of joy

_____

How could I have made today better

_____

1 Simple goal for tomorrow

_____

Date
_____/_____/_____

TODAY I AM GRATEFUL FOR

1. _____

2. _____

3. _____

TODAY I FEEL :   ☺   😐   ☹

How will I make today amazing ?

_____

_____

"Ardently do today what must be done. Who knows? Tomorrow, death comes."
- The Buddha

Todays moments of joy

_____

_____

How could I have made today better

_____

_____

1 Simple goal for tomorrow

_____

Date

____/____/____

TODAY I AM GRATEFUL FOR

1. _____

2. _____

3. _____

TODAY I FEEL :   ☺   😐   ☹

How will I make today amazing ?

_____

_____

"Your vision will become clear only when you look into your heart. Who looks outside, dreams. Who looks inside, awakens."
- Carl Jung

Todays moments of joy

_____

_____

How could I have made today better

_____

_____

1 Simple goal for tomorrow

Date

____/____/____

TODAY I AM GRATEFUL FOR

1.

2.

3.

TODAY I FEEL : ☺ 😐 ☹

How will I make today amazing ?

"Awareness is the greatest agent for change."
- Eckhart Tolle

Todays moments of joy

How could I have made today better

1 Simple goal for tomorrow

Date
____/____/____

TODAY I AM GRATEFUL FOR

1. _____
2. _____
3. _____

TODAY I FEEL : ☺ 😐 ☹

How will I make today amazing ?

_____
_____
_____

"Reality is only an agreement - today is always today."
- Zen Proverb

Todays moments of joy

_____

How could I have made today better

_____

1 Simple goal for tomorrow

_____

Date
_____/_____/_____

TODAY I AM GRATEFUL FOR

1. _____

2. _____

3. _____

TODAY I FEEL :   ☺   😐   ☹

How will I make today amazing ?

_____

_____

"The significance is hiding in the insignificant. Appreciate everything."
- **Eckhart Tolle**

Todays moments of joy

_____

How could I have made today better

_____

1 Simple goal for tomorrow

_____

Date
____/____/____

TODAY I AM GRATEFUL FOR

1. _____
2. _____
3. _____

TODAY I FEEL : ☺ 😐 ☹

Joyful affirmations

_____
_____
_____

"Throughout this life, you can never be certain of living long
enough to take another breath."
- Huang Po

Todays moments of joy

_____
_____

How could I have made today better

_____
_____

1 Simple goal for tomorrow

_____

Date
_____/_____/_____

TODAY I AM GRATEFUL FOR

1. _____
2. _____
3. _____

TODAY I FEEL :   ☺   😐   ☹

How will I make today amazing ?
Joyful affirmations

_____
_____
_____

"Be happy in the moment, that's enough. Each moment is all
we need, not more."
- Mother Teresa

Todays moments of joy
_____
_____

How could I have made today better
_____
_____

1 Simple goal for tomorrow
_____

My goals for the next 90 days

_____

_____

_____

_____

_____

_____

_____

_____

_____

_____

My thoughts and plans

_____

_____

_____

_____

_____

_____

_____

My goals for month 2

How will I make today amazing ?

'Believe you can and you're halfway there'
Theodore Roosevelt

How I will improve myself

Something fun I will do this month

Date
_____/_____/_____

TODAY I AM GRATEFUL FOR

1. _____
2. _____
3. _____

TODAY I FEEL :   ☺   😐   ☹

How will I make today amazing ?

_____
_____

"It is not enough to be busy... The question is: what are we busy about?"
Henry David Thoreau

Todays moments of joy

_____
_____

How could I have made today better

_____
_____

1 Simple goal for tomorrow

_____

Date
_____ / _____ / _____

TODAY I AM GRATEFUL FOR

1. _____
2. _____
3. _____

TODAY I FEEL : ☺ 😐 ☹

How will I make today amazing ?

_____

_____

"Your mind is for having ideas, not holding them."
David Allen

Todays moments of joy

_____

_____

How could I have made today better

_____

_____

1 Simple goal for tomorrow

_____

Date
____/____/____

TODAY I AM GRATEFUL FOR

1. _____
2. _____
3. _____

TODAY I FEEL :   😊   😐   ☹️

How will I make today amazing ?

_____
_____

"Nothing is less productive than to make more efficient what should not be done at all."
Peter Drucker

Todays moments of joy

_____
_____

How could I have made today better

_____
_____

1 Simple goal for tomorrow

_____

Date
____/____/____

TODAY I AM GRATEFUL FOR

1. _____

2. _____

3. _____

TODAY I FEEL :   ☺   😐   ☹

How will I make today amazing ?

_____

_____

"Success is often achieved by those who don't know that failure is inevitable."
Coco Chanel

Todays moments of joy

_____

How could I have made today better

_____

1 Simple goal for tomorrow

_____

Date
_____/_____/_____

TODAY I AM GRATEFUL FOR

1. _____
2. _____
3. _____

TODAY I FEEL : ☺   😐   ☹

How will I make today amazing ?

_____
_____

"We have only now, only this single eternal moment
opening and unfolding before us, day and night."
Jack Kornfield

Todays moments of joy

_____
_____

How could I have made today better

_____
_____

1 Simple goal for tomorrow

_____

Date
____/____/____

TODAY I AM GRATEFUL FOR

1. _____
2. _____
3. _____

TODAY I FEEL : ☺   😐   ☹

How will I make today amazing ?

_____
_____

"Perfection of character is this: to live each day as if it were your last, without frenzy, without apathy, without pretense."
- Marcus Aurelius, Meditations

Todays moments of joy

_____

How could I have made today better

_____

1 Simple goal for tomorrow

_____

Date
____/____/____

TODAY I AM GRATEFUL FOR

1. _____
2. _____
3. _____

TODAY I FEEL :   ☺   😐   ☹

How will I make today amazing ?

_____
_____

"Guilt, regret, resentment, sadness & all forms of nonforgive-
ness are caused by too much past & not enough presence."
- Eckhart Tolle

Todays moments of joy

_____
_____

How could I have made today better

_____
_____

1 Simple goal for tomorrow

Date
____/____/____

TODAY I AM GRATEFUL FOR

1. _____

2. _____

3. _____

TODAY I FEEL :   ☺   😐   ☹

How will I make today amazing ?

_____

_____

"Mindfulness, the Root of Happiness"
- Joseph Goldstein

Todays moments of joy

_____

How could I have made today better

_____

1 Simple goal for tomorrow

_____

Date
____/____/____

TODAY I AM GRATEFUL FOR

1. _____
2. _____
3. _____

TODAY I FEEL :   ☺   😐   ☹

How will I make today amazing ?

_____
_____

"The real voyage of discovery consists not in seeking out new landscapes but in having new eyes."
- Marcel Proust

Todays moments of joy

_____
_____

How could I have made today better

_____
_____

1 Simple goal for tomorrow

_____

Date

____/____/____

TODAY I AM GRATEFUL FOR

1. _____

2. _____

3. _____

TODAY I FEEL :   ☺   😐   ☹

How will I make today amazing ?

_____

_____

"The key is not to prioritize what's on your schedule, but to schedule your priorities."

Stephen Covey

Todays moments of joy

_____

_____

How could I have made today better

_____

_____

1 Simple goal for tomorrow

_____

Date
____ / ____ / ____

TODAY I AM GRATEFUL FOR

1. _____
2. _____
3. _____

TODAY I FEEL :   ☺   😐   ☹

How will I make today amazing ?

_____
_____

"Ordinary people think merely of spending time, great people think of using it."
Arthur Schopenhauer

Todays moments of joy

_____
_____

How could I have made today better

_____
_____

1 Simple goal for tomorrow

_____

Date
____/____/____

TODAY I AM GRATEFUL FOR

1. _____

2. _____

3. _____

TODAY I FEEL : ☺ 😐 ☹

How will I make today amazing ?

_____

_____

_____

"Time is the scarcest resource and unless it is managed nothing else can be managed"
Peter Drucker

Todays moments of joy

_____

_____

How could I have made today better

_____

_____

1 Simple goal for tomorrow

_____

Date
____/____/____

TODAY I AM GRATEFUL FOR

1. _____
2. _____
3. _____

TODAY I FEEL :   ☺   😐   ☹

How will I make today amazing ?

_____
_____
_____

"Focus on being productive instead of busy."
Tim Ferriss

Todays moments of joy

_____
_____

How could I have made today better

_____
_____

1 Simple goal for tomorrow

Date

____/____/____

TODAY I AM GRATEFUL FOR

1. _____

2. _____

3. _____

TODAY I FEEL :   ☺   😐   ☹

How will I make today amazing ?

_____

_____

"Time is at once the most valuable and the most perishable of all our possessions"
John Randolph

Todays moments of joy

_____

How could I have made today better

_____

1 Simple goal for tomorrow

Date
____/____/____

TODAY I AM GRATEFUL FOR

1. _____
2. _____
3. _____

TODAY I FEEL :   ☺   😐   ☹

How will I make today amazing ?

_____
_____
_____

"Absorb what is useful, reject what is useless, add what is specifically your own."
Bruce Lee

Todays moments of joy

_____
_____

How could I have made today better

_____
_____

1 Simple goal for tomorrow

Date

____/____/____

TODAY I AM GRATEFUL FOR

1. _____

2. _____

3. _____

TODAY I FEEL : 🙂 😐 🙁

How will I make today amazing ?

_____

_____

_____

"Efficiency is doing better what is already being done."
Peter Drucker

Todays moments of joy

_____

_____

How could I have made today better

_____

_____

1 Simple goal for tomorrow

_____

Date
____/____/____

TODAY I AM GRATEFUL FOR

1. _____
2. _____
3. _____

TODAY I FEEL :   ☺   😐   ☹

How will I make today amazing ?

_____
_____
_____

"This is the real secret of life — to be completely engaged with what you are doing in the here and now. And instead of calling it work, realize it is play."-
Alan Watts

Todays moments of joy

_____
_____

How could I have made today better

_____
_____

1 Simple goal for tomorrow

_____

Date
_____/_____/_____

TODAY I AM GRATEFUL FOR

1. _____
2. _____
3. _____

TODAY I FEEL : ☺ 😐 ☹

How will I make today amazing ?

_____
_____

"The only way to live is by accepting each minute as an unrepeatable miracle."
- Tara Brach

Todays moments of joy

_____
_____

How could I have made today better

_____
_____

1 Simple goal for tomorrow

Date
____/____/____

TODAY I AM GRATEFUL FOR

1. _____
2. _____
3. _____

TODAY I FEEL :   ☺   😐   ☹

How will I make today amazing ?

_____
_____

"Today, you can decide to walk in freedom. You can choose
to walk differently. You can walk as a free person, enjoying
every step."
- Thich Nhat Hanh

Todays moments of joy

_____
_____

How could I have made today better

_____
_____

1 Simple goal for tomorrow

Date
_____/_____/_____

TODAY I AM GRATEFUL FOR

1. _____
2. _____
3. _____

TODAY I FEEL :   ☺   😐   ☹

How will I make today amazing ?

_____
_____
_____

"In today's rush, we all think too much — seek too much —
want too much — and forget about the joy of just being."
- Eckhart Tolle

Todays moments of joy

_____
_____

How could I have made today better

_____
_____

1 Simple goal for tomorrow

_____

Date
____/____/____

TODAY I AM GRATEFUL FOR

1. _____

2. _____

3. _____

TODAY I FEEL :　　😊　　😐　　☹️

How will I make today amazing ?

_____

_____

"Life is not lost by dying; life is lost minute by minute, day by
dragging day, in all the small uncaring ways."
- Stephen Vincent Benet

Todays moments of joy

_____

_____

How could I have made today better

_____

_____

1 Simple goal for tomorrow

Date
____/____/____

TODAY I AM GRATEFUL FOR

1. _____
2. _____
3. _____

TODAY I FEEL :   ☺   😐   ☹

How will I make today amazing ?

_____

_____

"I feel that luck is preparation meeting opportunity."
Oprah Winfrey

Todays moments of joy

_____

_____

How could I have made today better

_____

_____

1 Simple goal for tomorrow

Date

____/____/____

TODAY I AM GRATEFUL FOR

1. _____

2. _____

3. _____

TODAY I FEEL :   :)   :| :(

How will I make today amazing ?

_____

_____

"Effective performance is preceded by painstaking preparation"

Brian Tracy

Todays moments of joy

_____

_____

How could I have made today better

_____

_____

1 Simple goal for tomorrow

_____

Date
_____/_____/_____

TODAY I AM GRATEFUL FOR

1. _____

2. _____

3. _____

TODAY I FEEL : ☺ 😐 ☹

How will I make today amazing ?

_____

_____

"The desire of knowledge, like the thirst for riches, increases
ever with the acquisition of it."
Laurence Sterne

Todays moments of joy

_____

_____

How could I have made today better

_____

_____

1 Simple goal for tomorrow

_____

Date

____/____/____

TODAY I AM GRATEFUL FOR

1. _____

2. _____

3. _____

TODAY I FEEL :   ☺   😐   ☹

How will I make today amazing ?

_____

_____

"The great accomplishments of man have resulted from the transmission of ideas of enthusiasm."
Thomas J. Watson

Todays moments of joy

_____

_____

How could I have made today better

_____

_____

1 Simple goal for tomorrow

Date
____/____/____

TODAY I AM GRATEFUL FOR

1. _____
2. _____
3. _____

TODAY I FEEL :   ☺   😐   ☹

How will I make today amazing ?

_____
_____

"Don't confuse the urgent with the important."
Preston Ni

Todays moments of joy

_____

How could I have made today better

_____

1 Simple goal for tomorrow

_____

Date
____/____/____

TODAY I AM GRATEFUL FOR

1. _____
2. _____
3. _____

TODAY I FEEL : 😊   😐   ☹️

How will I make today amazing ?

_____
_____

"What would it be like if I could accept life--accept this moment--exactly as it is?"
- Tara Brach

Todays moments of joy

_____
_____

How could I have made today better

_____
_____

1 Simple goal for tomorrow

Date

_____/_____/_____

TODAY I AM GRATEFUL FOR

1.

2.

3.

TODAY I FEEL :   😊   😐   ☹️

How will I make today amazing ?

"Everything is created twice, first in the mind and then in reality."

- Robin S. Sharma

Todays moments of joy

How could I have made today better

1 Simple goal for tomorrow

Date
____/____/____

TODAY I AM GRATEFUL FOR

1. _____
2. _____
3. _____

TODAY I FEEL : ☺ 😐 ☹

How will I make today amazing ?

_____
_____
_____

"Mindfulness, also called wise attention, helps us see what we're adding to our experiences, not only during meditation sessions but also elsewhere."
Sharon Salzberg

Todays moments of joy

_____
_____

How could I have made today better

_____
_____

1 Simple goal for tomorrow

_____

Date
____/____/____

TODAY I AM GRATEFUL FOR

1. _____
2. _____
3. _____

TODAY I FEEL :   ☺   😐   ☹

How will I make today amazing ?

_____
_____

"We use mindfulness to observe the way we cling to pleasant experiences & push away unpleasant ones."
Sharon Salzberg

Todays moments of joy

_____

How could I have made today better

_____
_____

1 Simple goal for tomorrow

Date
_____ / _____ / _____

TODAY I AM GRATEFUL FOR

1. _____
2. _____
3. _____

TODAY I FEEL : ☺ 😐 ☹

How will I make today amazing ?

_____
_____

"It's not about approving or liking, but just being able to allow the world to be the way it is without resenting, hating, or judging it."
- Buddhism Now

Todays moments of joy

_____
_____

How could I have made today better

_____
_____

1 Simple goal for tomorrow

_____

Date
____/____/____

TODAY I AM GRATEFUL FOR

1. _____

2. _____

3. _____

TODAY I FEEL : ☺ 😐 ☹

How will I make today amazing ?

_____

_____

_____

"When you are present, you can allow the mind to be as it is without getting entangled in it."
- Eckhart Tolle

Todays moments of joy

_____

_____

How could I have made today better

_____

_____

1 Simple goal for tomorrow

_____

My goals for the next 90 days

My thoughts and plans

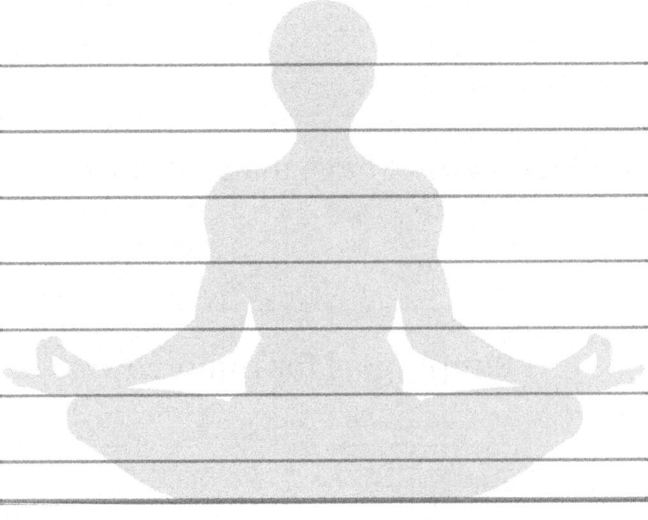

THIS MONTHS PLAN

My goals for month 3

'Believe you can and you're halfway there'
Theodore Roosevelt

How I will improve myself

Something fun I will do this month

Date
____/____/____

TODAY I AM GRATEFUL FOR

1. _____
2. _____
3. _____

TODAY I FEEL : ☺ 😐 ☹

How will I make today amazing ?

_____
_____

"We cannot be present and run our story-line at the same time."
Pema Chödrön

Todays moments of joy

_____
_____

How could I have made today better

_____
_____

1 Simple goal for tomorrow

Date
_____/_____/_____

TODAY I AM GRATEFUL FOR

1. _____
2. _____
3. _____

TODAY I FEEL :　　😊　　😐　　☹️

How will I make today amazing ?

_____
_____

"Every problem perceived to be 'out there' is really nothing
more than a misperception within your own thinking."
Byron Katie

Todays moments of joy

_____
_____

How could I have made today better

_____
_____

1 Simple goal for tomorrow

_____

Date
____ / ____ / ____

TODAY I AM GRATEFUL FOR

1. _____
2. _____
3. _____

TODAY I FEEL :   ☺   😐   ☹

How will I make today amazing ?

_____
_____

"Both good and bad days should end with productivity. You mood affairs should never influence your work."
Greg Evans

Todays moments of joy

_____
_____

How could I have made today better

_____
_____

1 Simple goal for tomorrow

Date
____/____/____

TODAY I AM GRATEFUL FOR

1. _____
2. _____
3. _____

TODAY I FEEL :   ☺   😐   ☹

How will I make today amazing ?

_____
_____
_____

"Efficiency is doing things right. Effectiveness is doing the right things."
Peter Drucker

Todays moments of joy

_____
_____

How could I have made today better

_____
_____

1 Simple goal for tomorrow

_____

Date
____/____/____

TODAY I AM GRATEFUL FOR

1. _____
2. _____
3. _____

TODAY I FEEL : ☺   😐   ☹

How will I make today amazing ?

_____
_____

"You don't need a new plan for next year. You need a commitment."
Seth Godin

Todays moments of joy

_____
_____

How could I have made today better

_____
_____

1 Simple goal for tomorrow

_____

Date
____/____/____

TODAY I AM GRATEFUL FOR

1. _____
2. _____
3. _____

TODAY I FEEL :   ☺   😐   ☹

How will I make today amazing ?

_____

_____

"To the degree we're not living our dreams; our comfort zone has more control of us than we have over ourselves."
Peter McWilliams

Todays moments of joy

_____

_____

How could I have made today better

_____

_____

1 Simple goal for tomorrow

Date
____/____/____

TODAY I AM GRATEFUL FOR

1. _____
2. _____
3. _____

TODAY I FEEL :   🙂   😐   🙁

How will I make today amazing ?

_____
_____

"If there are nine rabbits on the ground, if you want to catch one, just focus on one."
Jack Ma

Todays moments of joy

_____
_____

How could I have made today better

_____
_____

1 Simple goal for tomorrow

Date

____/____/____

TODAY I AM GRATEFUL FOR

1. _____
2. _____
3. _____

TODAY I FEEL :   ☺   😐   ☹

How will I make today amazing ?

_____

_____

"When one has much to put into them, a day has a hundred pockets."
Friedrich Nietzsche

Todays moments of joy

_____

_____

How could I have made today better

_____

_____

1 Simple goal for tomorrow

Date
____/____/____

1. _____
2. _____
3. _____

TODAY I FEEL :   ☺   😐   ☹

How will I make today amazing ?

_____
_____

"Surviving a failure gives you more self-confidence. Failures are great learning tools.. but they must be kept to a minimum."
Jeffrey Immelt

Todays moments of joy

_____
_____

How could I have made today better

_____
_____

1 Simple goal for tomorrow

Date
____/____/____

TODAY I AM GRATEFUL FOR

1. _____
2. _____
3. _____

TODAY I FEEL :   ☺   😐   ☹

How will I make today amazing ?

_____
_____

"A life spent making mistakes is not only more honorable, but more useful than a life spent doing nothing"
George Bernard Shaw

Todays moments of joy

_____

How could I have made today better

_____

1 Simple goal for tomorrow

Date
____/____/____

TODAY I AM GRATEFUL FOR

1. _____
2. _____
3. _____

TODAY I FEEL :   ☺   😐   ☹

How will I make today amazing ?

_____
_____
_____

"Working on the right thing is probably more important than working hard."
Caterina Fake

Todays moments of joy

_____
_____

How could I have made today better

_____
_____

1 Simple goal for tomorrow

_____

Date
____/____/____

TODAY I AM GRATEFUL FOR

1. _____

2. _____

3. _____

TODAY I FEEL :   ☺   😐   ☹

How will I make today amazing ?

_____

_____

"Follow effective actions with quiet reflection. From the quiet reflection will come even more effective action."
Peter Drucker

Todays moments of joy

_____

_____

How could I have made today better

_____

_____

1 Simple goal for tomorrow

_____

Date
____/____/____

TODAY I AM GRATEFUL FOR

1. _____
2. _____
3. _____

TODAY I FEEL :   ☺   😐   ☹

How will I make today amazing ?

_____
_____

"Few of us ever live in the present. We are forever anticipating what is to come or remembering what has gone."
Louis L'Amour

Todays moments of joy

_____
_____

How could I have made today better

_____
_____

1 Simple goal for tomorrow

Date
____/____/____

TODAY I AM GRATEFUL FOR

1. _____

2. _____

3. _____

TODAY I FEEL : ☺ 😐 ☹

How will I make today amazing ?

_____

_____

"If you want to conquer the anxiety of life, live in the moment, live in the breath."-
Amit Ray

Todays moments of joy

_____

_____

How could I have made today better

_____

_____

1 Simple goal for tomorrow

Date
____/____/____

TODAY I AM GRATEFUL FOR

1. _____
2. _____
3. _____

TODAY I FEEL : ☺ 😐 ☹

How will I make today amazing ?

_____
_____
_____

"If you aren't in the moment, you are either looking forward
to uncertainty, or back to pain and regret."
Jim Carrey

Todays moments of joy

_____
_____

How could I have made today better

_____
_____

1 Simple goal for tomorrow

Date
____/____/____

TODAY I AM GRATEFUL FOR

1. _____

2. _____

3. _____

TODAY I FEEL :   ☺   😐   ☹

How will I make today amazing ?

_____

_____

"All beings want to be happy, yet so very few know how. It is out of ignorance that any of us cause suffering, for ourselves or for others"
- Sharon Salzberg

Todays moments of joy

_____

_____

How could I have made today better

_____

_____

1 Simple goal for tomorrow

_____

Date
____/____/____

TODAY I AM GRATEFUL FOR

1. _____
2. _____
3. _____

TODAY I FEEL : ☺ 😐 ☹

How will I make today amazing ?

_____
_____

"The energy of mindfulness has the element of friendship
and loving kindness in it."
- Thich Nhat Hanh

Todays moments of joy

_____
_____

How could I have made today better

_____
_____

1 Simple goal for tomorrow

_____

Date
____/____/____

TODAY I AM GRATEFUL FOR

1. _____
2. _____
3. _____

TODAY I FEEL : ☺ 😐 ☹

How will I make today amazing ?

_____
_____

"Look at other people and ask yourself if you are really seeing them or just your thoughts about them."
Jon Kabat-Zinn

Todays moments of joy

_____

How could I have made today better

_____

1 Simple goal for tomorrow

_____

Date
_____/_____/_____

TODAY I AM GRATEFUL FOR

1. _____
2. _____
3. _____

TODAY I FEEL : ☺ 😐 ☹

How will I make today amazing ?

_____
_____

"We often have very little empathy for our own thoughts and feelings and frequently try to suppress them by dismissing them as weaknesses."
- Mark Williams

Todays moments of joy

_____
_____

How could I have made today better

_____
_____

1 Simple goal for tomorrow

Date
____/____/____

TODAY I AM GRATEFUL FOR

1. _____
2. _____
3. _____

TODAY I FEEL :   ☺   😐   ☹

How will I make today amazing ?

_____
_____

"The most precious gift we can offer others is our presence. When mindfulness embraces those we love, they will bloom like flowers."-
Thich Nhat Hanh

Todays moments of joy

_____
_____

How could I have made today better

_____
_____

1 Simple goal for tomorrow

_____

Date
____/____/____

TODAY I AM GRATEFUL FOR

1. _____

2. _____

3. _____

TODAY I FEEL :   ☺   😐   ☹

How will I make today amazing ?

_____

_____

"There is no substitute for hard work."
Thomas Edison

Todays moments of joy

_____

_____

How could I have made today better

_____

_____

1 Simple goal for tomorrow

Date

____/____/____

TODAY I AM GRATEFUL FOR

1. _____

2. _____

3. _____

TODAY I FEEL :   ☺   😐   ☹

How will I make today amazing ?

_____

_____

"Action is the foundational key to all success."
Picasso

Todays moments of joy

_____

_____

How could I have made today better

_____

_____

1 Simple goal for tomorrow

_____

Date
____/____/____

TODAY I AM GRATEFUL FOR

1. _____

2. _____

3. _____

TODAY I FEEL : ☺ 😐 ☹

How will I make today amazing ?

_____

_____

"Never mistake motion for action."
Ernest Hemingway

Todays moments of joy

_____

_____

How could I have made today better

_____

_____

1 Simple goal for tomorrow

_____

Date

____/____/____

TODAY I AM GRATEFUL FOR

1. _____

2. _____

3. _____

TODAY I FEEL : ☺ 😐 ☹

How will I make today amazing ?

_____

_____

_____

"While one person hesitates because he feels inferior, the other is busy making mistakes and becoming superior."
Henry Link

Todays moments of joy

_____

_____

How could I have made today better

_____

_____

1 Simple goal for tomorrow

_____

Date
____/____/____

1.

2.

3.

TODAY I FEEL :   ☺   😐   ☹

How will I make today amazing ?

"No matter how great the talent or efforts, some things just take time. You can't produce a baby in one month by getting nine women pregnant."
Warren Buffett

Todays moments of joy

How could I have made today better

1 Simple goal for tomorrow

Date
_____/_____/_____

TODAY I AM GRATEFUL FOR

1. _____

2. _____

3. _____

TODAY I FEEL : ☺ ☻ ☹

How will I make today amazing ?

_____

_____

"My goal is no longer to get more done, but rather to have less to do."
Francine Jay

Todays moments of joy

_____

_____

How could I have made today better

_____

_____

1 Simple goal for tomorrow

_____

Date
____/____/____

TODAY I AM GRATEFUL FOR

1. _____
2. _____
3. _____

TODAY I FEEL :   ☺   😐   ☹

How will I make today amazing ?

_____
_____

"Improved productivity means less human sweat, not more."
Henry Ford

Todays moments of joy

_____
_____

How could I have made today better

_____
_____

1 Simple goal for tomorrow

Date
____/____/____

TODAY I AM GRATEFUL FOR

1. _____
2. _____
3. _____

TODAY I FEEL : ☺ 😐 ☹

How will I make today amazing ?

_____
_____

"The noblest search is the search for excellence."
Lyndon B. Johnson

Todays moments of joy

_____
_____

How could I have made today better

_____
_____

1 Simple goal for tomorrow

_____

Date

____/____/____

TODAY I AM GRATEFUL FOR

1. _____

2. _____

3. _____

TODAY I FEEL :   ☺   😐   ☹

How will I make today amazing ?

_____

_____

_____

"It's not always that we need to do more but rather that we need to focus on less."
Nathan W. Morris

Todays moments of joy

_____

_____

How could I have made today better

_____

_____

1 Simple goal for tomorrow

_____

Date

____/____/____

TODAY I AM GRATEFUL FOR

1. _____

2. _____

3. _____

TODAY I FEEL : ☺ 😐 ☹

How will I make today amazing ?

_____

_____

"You must remain focused on your journey to greatness."
Les Brown

Todays moments of joy

_____

_____

How could I have made today better

_____

_____

1 Simple goal for tomorrow

_____

Made in the USA
Coppell, TX
02 December 2021

66953489R00057